HUNTINGDON
A Pictorial History

An aerial view of Huntingdon in 1966. At this time the government offices in Chequers Court were under construction. Today the St Benedict's shopping development occupies the site between the old Hippodrome cinema car park and the old council yard. (Photograph courtesy of the *Peterborough Evening Telegraph.*

HUNTINGDON
A Pictorial History

David Cozens

Phillimore

1995

Published by
PHILLIMORE & CO. LTD.
Shopwyke Manor Barn, Chichester, West Sussex

ISBN 0 85033 997 9

Printed and bound in Great Britain by
BIDDLES LTD.
Guildford, Surrey

Dedication

The book is dedicated to the Life President of the Huntingdonshire Local History Society, the Rt. Hon. Lord Renton K.B.E., Q.C., D.L. In 1945 David Renton was elected Member of Parliament for Huntingdonshire and served the constituency for 34 years. Sitting in the House of Lords since 1979, he has now been involved in national politics for 50 years.

List of Illustrations

Frontispiece: Aerial photograph of Huntingdon, 1966

Acknowledgements

How is it that a timetable which appeared quite reasonable at the start seemed to require increasingly more time as the deadline approached? First and foremost I wish to thank Mary, my wife, for her forbearance as domestic routines became increasingly disrupted.

Philip Saunders and Lesley James in the County Record Office at Huntingdon have been especially helpful in providing answers to many questions and by making the photographic material readily available for selection.

The majority of the illustrations cover approximately 100 years from the 1850s and were the work of three photographers who are the subject of the first chapter. In the 1970s Tim Crane in Cambridge used some of the early negatives to produce excellent positive prints. More recently Ron Bailey in Huntingdon and even more so John Critchley in Ramsey stepped in to 'save the day' when I had to change my arrangements for printing many of the secondary negatives.

I would like to thank all those people who have contributed to this pictorial history by sharing with me their knowledge of specific subjects or events. I trust that I have accurately transmitted their information together with that gathered from many written sources.

Sources consulted include:
Corbett, F.J. (ed.) *The Huntingdonshire Coronation Souvenir* (1911)
Dickinson, P.G.M., *Historic Huntingdon* (1944)
Dickinson, P.G.M., *Huntingdon Town Guides* (1950-69)
Dickinson, P.G.M. and Jamieson, A., *The History of Huntingdon Grammar School* (1965)
Dunn, C., *The Book of Huntingdon* (1977)
Hatfield, J., *History Gazetteer and Directory of the County of Huntingdon* (1854)
Page, W. (ed.), *The Victoria History of the County of Huntingdon* (1932)
Records of Huntingdonshire (1965-1995)
Saunders, W.H.B. (ed.), *Memorials of Godmanchester. Reminisces of F.W. Bird* (1911)
Threlfall, J.H., *The Story of Huntingdon County Hospital* (1980)

The endpapers are taken from *The Huntingdonshire Coronation Souvenir* of 1911.

Introduction

Twenty-five years ago several members of the Huntingdonshire Local History Society were asked to examine the contents of a cellar in Ermine Street, Huntingdon. We discovered, buried beneath the dust and rubble, that had fallen through the floor during the demolition of the building overhead, many glass plates stacked one upon the other. We were obviously in a cellar that had been used to store photographic negatives in the days when the photo-sensitive emulsions were supported on sheets of glass. Unfortunately the majority of the plates were badly damaged and beyond recovery.

We were disappointed and it seemed that this would be the end of the story, but we were mistaken. This subterranean excursion proved to be the beginning of a project on the work of three photographers who from the 1860s to the 1950s recorded life in and around Huntingdon. The project also revealed commercial rivalry from across the river in Godmanchester.

The three photographers were Arthur Maddison, Frederick Hinde, and Ernest Whitney.

Ernest Whitney in retirement and a member of the Local History Society, on hearing of our endeavours in the Ermine Street cellar, invited me to his home in Hartford. He thought that I might be interested in the material that he had saved

1   The cellar of 74 Ermine Street.

from the Huntingdon studio. He had retained just over 300 plates measuring 9-10ins. x 12ins. (22-24mm x 30mm) and approximately 650 smaller plates measuring 5½ins. x 7¼ins. (14mm x 18mm). In addition there were about 300 positive paper print of various sizes and 150 photographic magic lantern slides. I spent many hours taking notes in the little wooden shed that had once been his workplace, as Ernest identified the subjects captured on the negatives and prints. He ruefully recalled the commercial pressures associated with management of the studio that had caused him, many years ago, to send large numbers of glass plate negatives to the refuse tip. The material he rescued is now in the safe keeping of the County Record Office in Huntingdon. The collection provides the majority of illustrations reproduced in this pictorial history.

It is not possible to determine how selective Ernest was in making his collection but it appears that the earliest photographs were commissioned by the more affluent members of society. Early portraits include those of the aristocracy, and those of public figures. Local businessmen and their families were also early subjects. It is interesting to note that in the 1870s and at the other end of the social spectrum the county authorities were photographing the inmates of the prison. Some of the wealthy families commissioned photographs of their domestic servants who could number as many as thirty-five, as at Hinchingbrooke in 1909.

Public events were recorded and many local people were photographed when gathered together for weddings or in family, school or church groups. Others were photographed in costume taking part in theatrical events, or in uniform as members of the Police Force or the Fire Brigade. The community at play was captured in photographs showing various country pursuits and team sports.

During the working lives of our three photographers Huntingdon was the administrative centre of a largely agricultural area yet there were other commercial interests and many of these are illustrated. The photographs record countryside that now contains industrial units or new houses, residential buildings in the town that are now converted to offices, gardens that now contain offices and car parks. The photographers recorded High Street shops that have since changed hands or been demolished and replaced.

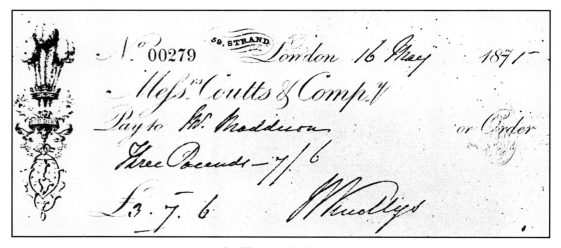

2 The royal cheque.

Photographers by Royal Appointment

The first section of this book is devoted to the photographers, their studios and their promotional activities.

Arthur Maddison was born in St Neots, Huntingdonshire in 1833. He acquired his photographic training in Bedford. In 1854, and giving his address as Huntingdon, he described in the *Journal of the Photographic Society* a technique for the production of positive images using waxed black paper and Archer's collodion emulsion. Five years later he was advertising his 'Superior Collodion and Varnish', giving the formula for the latter in the *Journal* in 1861. His claim to have produced a superior varnish is vindicated by the excellent condition of his surviving negatives. He exhibited to the Royal Photographic Society and was commended for the great accuracy of delineation of his work produced with Dallmeyer's new triple achromatic lens. In 1868, hearing that the Prince of Wales would be visiting the Duke of Manchester at Kimbolton Castle, he offered to record the royal visit. At this time his notepaper was headed 'Artist and Photographer', Huntingdon and Bedford. The offer was accepted, and the Duke's secretary advised Mr. Maddison that 'the photographs are much approved of' and enclosed orders from the Prince of Wales, the Duke of Sutherland, the Duchess of Manchester, the Earl of Westmorland, The Countess of Listowell, Viscountess Dangan, Lords Proby and Bingham, and Colonel Keppel. From then on Arthur proclaimed his appointment as Royal Photographer and incorporated the Prince of Wales' Feathers into the artwork on the back of his *carte-de-visite* prints.

At the age of 41 he married Julia Hinde, a 37-year-old widow who bore him three children. On Arthur's death in 1887 his son Cecil and his step-son **Frederick Hinde** continued his business, operating as Maddison and Hinde. In the mid-1890s the connection with Bedford was maintained through the Hinde and Carpenter studio. Cecil emigrated to Canada and Frederick concentrated his efforts upon the Ermine Street studio, earning a reputation as an excellent portrait photographer. Mr. Hinde and his mother were active members of the nonconformist Trinity church in Huntingdon and reputedly on a Sunday in 1906 Frederick refused to take a photograph even though the subject was King Edward VII. The King was being entertained at Hinchingbrooke House by the 8th Earl of Sandwich. Frederick died in 1927 and his widow Maude sold the contents of the Huntingdon and the St Ives studios to Ernest Whitney.

Ernest Whitney had joined Mr. Hinde in 1903 as a 14-year-old boy, working for him for six to seven years, before striking out on his own. Photographs taken by E.S. Whitney of Hartford were published in the *Huntingdonshire Coronation Souvenir* produced in 1911. During the First World War Ernest served as a photographer with the Royal Flying Corps and when Charles Barnard visited Huntingdon in the 1930s Ernest produced a series of aerial photographs. Later Ernest Whitney was advertising from his 'Electric Studio' in Huntingdon and was established at the opposite end of the town from the original Ermine Street premises. Ernest also had occasion to photograph royalty through his connection with the Papworth Hospital. In the late 1970s Ernest and his wife Eve emigrated to New Zealand to join their daughter.

Although the majority of the photographs reproduced in this book originated from the studios of these three photographers, Maddison, Hinde and Whitney were not the only professionals working in and around Huntingdon during this period. It is clear that there was intense rivalry from **Alfred Hendry** who was born in Huntingdon in 1853 and who set up studios in Godmanchester in 1872. On the reverse of his photographs Alfred stated that he was 'photographer to their Royal Highnesses the Prince and Princess of Wales'. This caused Arthur Maddison to accuse him of 'deceiving and imposing upon the public since he, Arthur Maddison, was the only photographer in the county to be honoured by command of their Royal Highnesses the Prince and Princess of Wales'.

After Arthur's death Frederick Hinde continued to advertise 'The Royal Art Studio' in Ermine Street. Alfred Hendry responded by claiming 'there was no Royal Studio in Huntingdon, and that it was all moonshine'. Furthermore in 1904 Alfred was making it known that he did not use inexperienced boys. Did he have in mind the likes of Ernest Whitney? On Frederick Hinde's alleged refusal to work on a Sunday it was Alfred Hendry's work that 'delighted His Majesty King Edward VII' from then on clearly entitling the Hendry studio to advertise its 'Royal connections'. Alfred met an untimely death in 1910. Examples of his photographic prints are rare although the quality of his work is evident in the postcards he produced between 1903 and 1910.

3 Arthur and Julia Maddison. Arthur was born at St Neots in 1833, the year that Talbot began his attempts to use light to make permanent images. Six years later Talbot and Daguerre revealed their different techniques to the general public. In 1851 Scott Archer announced the wet plate method which Arthur subsequently used in Huntingdon.

4 Arthur established his photographic studio in this property in Ermine Street. A later photograph shows the low range modified to give a uniform roof line bereft of dormers. In the distance can be seen the sign of *The White Horse* and just in view is the cobbled entrance to *The Rose and Crown*.

5 Although this image is badly damaged it shows Mr. Maddison supervising the construction of his studio. The large windows were essential in the days when the initial exposure and subsequent printing depended upon daylight. Even in 1903 enlargement was effected by passing light through the negative placed in a box on the roof of the dark room!

6 Through the good offices of Mr. Valentine Hill, the secretary to the Duke of Manchester, Arthur was able to photograph the Prince of Wales during visits to Kimbolton Castle. This photograph appears to have been taken in March 1870 during a week spent at the steeple-chase, at various hunts and at the ball for the Duke's Light Horse of which the Prince was the Honorary Colonel.

7 Between 1887 and 1927 Arthur's stepson Frederick Hinde ran the business in a conservative manner, continuing the old skills. This photograph was taken in 1904 by Ernest Whitney. Mr. Hinde is shown sitting in the studio with its painted backcloths, its furniture and the blinds to control the light.

8 In July 1906 King Edward VII visited the Earl of Sandwich at Huntingdon. It is understood that Mr. Hinde declined to work on a Sunday and this photograph was taken by Alfred Hendry of Godmanchester 'whose work delighted His Majesty'. (Photograph courtesy of Pauline Lord.)

9 Ernest Whitney launched out on his own, *c*.1910. The photograph shows him in his studio, which was also illuminated by daylight, but clearly smaller and less well furnished than the one in Ermine Street.

10 Arising from his association with the Papworth Hospital, Ernest was required on many occasions to photograph members of the Royal Family including George V, Edward VIII and George VI. This photograph reproduced from a lantern slide shows the Duke and Duchess of York with Sir Pendrill Varrier Jones.

The County Town

First recorded in the Anglo-Saxon Chronicle in the 650s 'Huntendune porte', Huntingdon, developed on an ancient trackway at its approach to the river Great Ouse. The 9th century saw the military and the peaceful presence of the Danes. In 921 Edward the Elder seized the town, fortified the burh and organised the surrounding area into a shire; soon afterwards a mint was established. In 1068 William the Conqueror erected the castle which survived until 1174. Huntingdon prospered until the 14th century when the Black Death killed a quarter of the population. This and the impaired navigation of the river led to the decline of the town. Matters were not improved when the religious houses were dissolved in the 16th century or by the Royal attack upon the town in the following century. With the advent of coach traffic in the 18th century Huntingdon was reinvigorated, only to decline again as the railway made the horse-drawn coach redundant. The North Road, however, remained a major route and in time the town became choked with motor vehicles. The town was essentially a linear development along the main road constrained within the encircling commons. It was not until the 19th century that building along the Brampton Road and the construction of Newtown began the process of expansion. In 1935 the village of Hartford was incorporated into the town. The 1960s saw the construction of Oxmoor beyond the commons. Recently the sale of Grammar School land has led to the development towards Great Stukeley, encouraged by the development of land belonging to St John's College, Cambridge. A significant proportion of the park surrounding 'the big house', that is Hinchingbrooke House, is also being developed. In the mid-19th century, when Arthur Maddison began taking his photographs in and around Huntingdon, the majority of the inhabitants lived in the parish of St Mary and St Benedict and in the parish of All Saints and St John. Today the centre of population is to be found outside the boundary of the old town. The upgrading and the realignment of the main roads around Huntingdon has reinforced the strategic position of the town with its close proximity to major east-west and north-south transport routes.

11   Taken in 1931, this aerial photograph was one of a series produced by Ernest Whitney. The main road from York enters the town from the north and then swings to the east of the castle to cross the river into Godmanchester. Noticeably absent is any development towards the Stukeleys or alongside the Great Northern Railway.

12   On 29 July 1931 Captain C.D. Barnard brought his Air Circus to Portholme. Barnard with the Duchess of Bedford had made record-breaking flights to and from India. An advertisement for the circus referred to Spartan and Potez machines, to 'The Spider' and to the Cierva Autogiro. Ernest with his camera became a passenger. This aerial photograph is signed by Barnard.

13 Looking down onto the High Street. Notable features include the garden of Castle Hill House, the Maddox works, Trinity church, Queen's Head Passage, the chimney of the brewery, the Town Hall and the ridge and furrow in the commonable land beyond the Walks North.

14 This Whitney aerial photograph of Godmanchester is included to show the alignment of Ermine Street, which is believed to have passed in front of the church, carried on beneath the circular flower bed and then continued in a straight line to the river bank opposite the site of Huntingdon Castle.

15 Returning to the beginning of the century and to ground level this shows the main road, the High Street, shortly after it enters the town from Godmanchester. Nowadays No. 151 High Street is without its shutters and further along *The Waterloo* has been built-up to two storeys. On the left numbers 9-12 are little changed.

16 Huntingdon once contained 16 churches, three religious houses and three hospitals; of these only two remain to serve their original purpose. St Mary's contains Norman work and a chancel and arcade from the 13th century. In 1607 part of the 14th-century tower collapsed; repairs were completed by 1620. Colonel Jonathan Peel and Thomas Baring, the two Members of Parliament for the Borough, provided the churchyard railings in 1863.

17 Castle Hill House was built in 1786 by Owsley Rowley. This photograph predates 1867. In 1977, before Pathfinder House was constructed, attempts were made to locate the remains of Ermine Street. The expected evidence was not found but a succession of Roman metalled surfaces was discovered at right angles to the anticipated line.

18 Taken in 1900, this photograph shows Mr. Markham's house positioned between St Mary's church and the vicarage. The building was once known as *The Bull Inn* and gave its name to the minor way Bull Lane. The lane was renamed Hartford Road when it replaced Germain Street as the main way to St Ives.

19 *The Bull* and St Mary's vicarage were demolished. This photograph taken in the 1940s shows a more familiar view; dominating the scene is the spire of Trinity church built in 1867, The photographic negative recording the foundation stone ceremony for the church was numbered, negatives bearing lower numbers can therefore be dated 'as early than 1867'.

20 This lantern slide shows a caterpillar tractor towing a workman's van negotiating the narrow road between Hartford Road and the High Street. *The Three Tuns* has recently been renamed *The Dog and Bone*.

21 Hartford Road being widened, *c*.1937. In 1899 George Maddox was set up in business by his former employer Charles Windover. George employed around 100 men making carriages and cars. In 1924 the factory, together with a car body being constructed for the Prime Minister of Australia's Rolls Royce, was destroyed by fire. It is now the site of Marshalls' Peugeot garage.

22 Trinity church was an impressive structure with a spire 180 feet in height. The figure stands on the pavement alongside 25 Hartford Road. The absence of the Montagu Club indicates that the photograph was taken before 1897, the year when the 8th Earl of Sandwich donated the building. One room was to be used for technical education and two rooms for a working men's club.

23 Mr. Colbon's house, photographed in 1902. The house frontage is almost hidden behind the vigorous wisterias. The property, apparently then called Newtown House, is now simply identified as 27 West Street, Huntingdon.

24 Looking towards Hartford from the footpath which once ran parallel to the Hartford Road before turning up to American Lane. Noticeably absent is the pump house and any evidence of residential development alongside Hartford Road.

25 Photographed in 1891, Mr. Newbury's house The Elms stood at the corner of Main Street and Sapley Road in Hartford. The property has been extended to the left but truncated to the right and now accommodates the Hartford Village Stores.

26 This photograph, taken between 1860 and 1870, was helpful in establishing the existence of a public right of way between the churchyard wall and the river. At this time *The Crown* abutted the churchyard. A chain ferry once linked The Hollow to the meadow across the river.

27 Alongside Walter Driver's shop was that of Edward Sarll, glass and china merchant. Edward's property bore an annual charge of 10 shillings to provide bread for the poor of St Mary's, as instituted by Thomas Woodward in 1720. Next was another shop, now the Bookshop, and beyond that Dr. Foster's house and the Literary and Scientific Institution established in 1842.

28 Visible to the left is the doorway into the Literary Passage and beyond Jacob's the Saddlers now the Parsley Pot. To the right can be seen Mr. Tatman's pork butcher shop and *The White Hart Inn*; these are now the premises of Tesco and the Alliance and Leicester Building Society. Hendry's advertisement looks down at the turn of the road.

29 Another more recent photograph showing *The Queen's Head* with its passage way and the direction sign to the borough council cycle park. *The Queen's Head* and the adjacent building were rebuilt to house the Abbey National Bank and the Premier Travel Agency; the properties beyond were demolished to form the entrance to St Benedict's Court.

30 Looking back down the High Street from today's Smith's shop. On the left is the 1869 brewery house with Trinity church spire beyond. On the right is *The Crown*, offering livery, billiards and stables. *The Crown*, in which Pepys recorded 'taking a breakfast of cold roast beef' and 'drinking ale until we were very merry', stood across the road.

31 On the right can be seen William Goggs' stationer, now Eastern Electricity and Currys. On the left is All Saints Passage and beyond Coxon's shop, once Mother Goode's coffee shop. On the corner of Market Hill is the Huntingdon Town and County Bank taken over by Barclays in 1896.

32   There are few shops in this photograph taken before 1892. To the left is Wykeham House, once the London and County Joint Stock Bank and the County Club. This 19th-century building is grafted onto *The Falcon Inn* which was used as a headquarters by Oliver Cromwell. The 17th-century Walden House lies alongside. Across the road from All Saints Church is the Grammar School.

33   The house of the architect Mr. Hutchinson photographed in the 1880s. In recent times the offices of the architects Milner and Roberts were in this house. In the 1970s these architects designed the Gazebo in St Benedict's Court incorporating some of the pillars from the butcher market seen on the right. The building to the left of the house is now the smoke room of *The Market Inn*.

34 This row of cottages in Princess Street was demolished to make way for the Waitrose Supermarket. Set into the wall of the cottages was a stone engraved 'Hugh Ferrar 1771'. The white building remains intact. The street was once gated at the entrance to Mill Common.

35 Photographed in 1899, this is recorded as Mrs. R. Ashton's drawing room, somewhat excessively furnished for today's taste. Kelly's *Directory* of 1898 records Mr. R. Ashton living at Lawrence Cottage, The Walks North, now demolished.

36 This photograph shows *The Queen's Head*, formerly *The Falcon*, with its passage leading on to the High Street. To the left of *The Queen's Head* was St Bennet's Passage. To the left again a range of buildings, one of which included a medieval open hall. All of these structures were demolished in 1977 and partially replaced to form St Benedict's Court.

37 One of the town's pumps was positioned at the George Street corner against the boundary wall of All Saints Church alongside the 1859 chamber for the church organ. The building was damaged when Charles I attacked Huntingdon in 1645 and the tower was reconstructed in brick. Ermine Street is thought to run beneath the church.

38 This interesting house with its mansard roof used to stand in George Street between the Church of St John the Evangelist and Sandford House. It no longer exists. Sandford House was home of C.S. Windover.

39 On the left the Carriage Works built by C.S. Windover and ahead is the outer yard of *The George Hotel*. The out-buildings were removed to improve access into the town.

40 The County Hospital was built in 1853 to replace the 1789 Dispensary and Infirmary on the Walks North. This picture was taken in 1895, a year which saw a matron 'recommended by Florence Nightingale' in dispute with the board regarding the training and status of the nurses!

41 Hinchingbrooke Gatehouse was constructed in the 16th century by Sir Henry Cromwell, the Golden Knight, at the entrance to the house being constructed from the nunnery. He used some of the fabric from the 15th-century gatehouse of Ramsey Abbey, which had also been acquired by the family at the dissolution of the monasteries. Photographed before 1867.

42 The present library was formed in the 1890s when an existing library was enlarged to incorporate all the remaining ground floor of the former church. The portrait of Jemima is at the far end and that of her husband, the 1st Earl of Sandwich, is shown on the right.

43 This dining room was constructed in 1894-6. It is appropriate to recall that 'The Sandwich' was invented by the 4th Earl who as a hard-working First Lord of the Admiralty did not wish to stop to eat a meal. Another explanation is that he chose not to waste time by eating a full meal when at the gambling table!

44 When Samuel Pepys visited Hinchingbrooke he used to walk on the terrace which lay behind this 'wall on the mount'. He was for a time secretary to 'My Lord' the 1st Earl. The road leading to Brampton crossed the Alconbury Brook at Nun's bridge. During the construction of the present bridge a roman burial was discovered.

45 This 1888 photograph of Brampton park is included because it was the home of Lady Olivia Bernard Sparrow, the founder of the church of St John the Evangelist in Huntingdon. John Nash was employed on the house between 1806 and 1808. Although the majority of the building was destroyed by fire in 1907, the remaining western range now forms the Officers' Mess at RAF Brampton.

46 Returning to the High Street we find Mr. Lamb coming towards us on his tricycle. On the corner of *The George Hotel* is Maddison and Hinde's display case. Lloyds Bank now occupies the site of the 18th-century house with its prominent doorway; it also incorporates part of the adjacent building. Photographed *c.*1910.

47 Coaches to Boston, Cambridge, Leicester, London, Northampton and Stamford once called here and in 1845 there were more than 100 horses in the stables. In 1887 the courtyard was covered for the Jubilee celebrations. Beneath the 17th-century wing, with its open gallery and staircase, is a Rover tourer EW 407. The courtyard makes a fine setting for the traditional summer-time productions of 'Shakespeare at *The George*'.

48 Just along the street is a better example of the passages previously encountered. This is the Royal Oak Passage showing the paved carriageway for the cartwheels. The passage has recently been renovated. To the left was once *The Royal Oak*, now being restored, while across the High Street are the premises of Cox County Clothiers, with Manchester Place alongside.

49 Ashton's Implement Store on the left is now Taylor's the Estate Agents, and just beyond is the 18th-century Falcon House associated with the Falcon Brewery, possibly the successor to Cromwell's Brewery. In the distance is the 19th-century Montagu House. Photographed before 1892.

50 This 1822 drawing by Tytler shows the 18th-century Ferrar House and trees in the churchyard of Oliver Cromwell's family church, the church of St John. In the distance is All Saints church, not yet obscured by the 1865 reconstruction of *The George Hotel*. Visible on the left is the gateway to Oliver's birthplace, to the right 18th-century Whitwell House.

51 Cromwell House was built upon the site of an Augustinian Friary, which in the 14th century was given permission to lay a conduit to carry water from the well called Caldewell, on Spring Common. During the 19th century Mr. Hutchinson designed a slipper bath which took its water from the spring. The photograph shows a family collecting water.

52 On the right is a terrace of 18th-century houses and beyond is *The Rose and Crown* with its tall chimney. In the middle distance is the studio of Maddison and Hinde. We have just crossed the town ditch once traversed by St Andrew's bridge leading to Balmshole. When Charles I attacked the town in 1645 he brushed aside defences erected at this point.

53 These almshouses, constructed in 1859, lay across the road from the site of the Leper Hospital of St Margaret founded outside the town in 1150. This once rural location now contains The Spittals roundabout and the Ermine business park.

Local Administration

The ancient borough of Huntingdon was privileged and largely independent of the sheriff. The privileges were codified in 1348 and in 1484 the corporate body was stated to be 'The Bailiff and Burgesses'. In 1630 this body was replaced by 'a mayor and twelve aldermen drawn from the better burgesses'. Oliver Cromwell objected to the 1630 Governing Charter and moved from Huntingdon to live in St Ives.

Dissatisfaction with the organisation of local government led to the Municipal Corporation Acts of 1835 and 1882. These Acts enfranchised the majority of the townsfolk giving the ratepayers the right to elect the town council.

Huntingdonshire was administered jointly with Cambridgeshire to the extent that for much of the time the two counties shared one sheriff. However it was the Justices of the Peace who, in addition to keeping the peace and dispensing justice, were from the 14th century required to attend to various aspects of civil administration. The administration became increasingly onerous, some of the business of the Quarter Sessions was delegated to committees, and eventually in 1888 the County Councils were formed.

At the time of writing Huntingdonshire Council is a district council within Cambridgeshire and Huntingdon is a tertiary council with a mayor! The following photographs show aspects of local government between 1870 and the 1960s.

54 The Guardians of the Law and Order photographed in 1912 at their 1881 headquarters in Ferrars Road. The county police had previously occupied premises on the High Street, which were eventually demolished to provide access to the new St Benedict's Court.

55 Mr. Whitney identified this as Horsford's trial. Walter Horsford of Spaldwick was found guilty of poisoning his cousin Annie Holmes. The trial took place in Huntingdon and he was executed by hanging in 1898.

56 This portrait accompanies the entry for Louisa Dickerson of Stilton in the Record Book of the County Gaol in St Peter's Road. In 1877, at the age of 19, she stole a watch valued at £3 and, this being a second offence, she was sentenced to four months' hard labour. The original records are in the Police Museum in Peterborough.

57 In 1950 Ernest Whitney, the mayor of Huntingdon, follows the judge in procession from All Saints Church to the Crown Court in the Town Hall. In the previous century the procession would have been attended by men carrying six-foot-long javelins and the judge would have attended St Mary's Church. The Crown Courts moved to Peterborough in 1980.

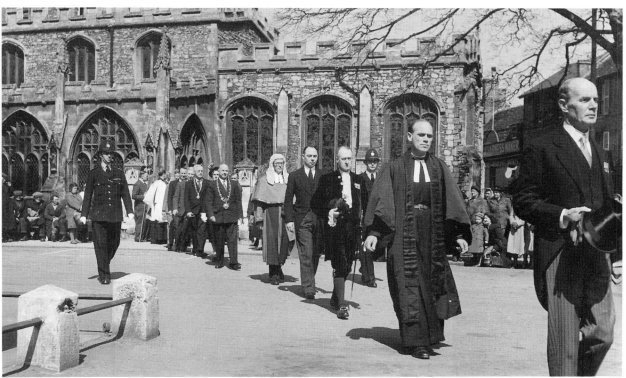

Top Row from L. to R.: W. K. Townson (Veterinary Officer), A. E. James (Inspector of Weights and Measures), W. W. Whittome, G. A. Earl, W. T. Cook, T. E. R. Parsons, C. H. Chandler, Rev. E. I. Evans, T. S. Christmas, D. M. Gibbins, G. E. Taylor, H. J. Poulter, W. P. Anderson, F. Chapman, J. H. Bradshaw, W. H. Gotobed, A. G. O. Ashpole (County Land Agent), S. J. Hands (County Architect).

Middle Row from L. to R.: T. H. Longstaff (County Surveyor), F. M. Warr (County Treasurer), Miss O. D. Clarke (Children's Officer), E. G. Holmes, H. Wicks, G. E. Fuller, B. S. Bye, F. C. Slaughter, G. H. Johnson, Sir R. G. Proby, Bt., The Rt. Hon. The Lord Hemingford, J. J. Wilkins, C. M. J. Coote, R. H. Shelley, G. R. F. Rowley, O. N. D. Sismey, L. J. W. Barker, R. Osborn, J. G. Ellis (Welfare Officer), I. C. Currey (Director of Education), Dr. D. S. Buchanan (County Medical Officer), A. Easton (Chief Fire Officer).

Front Row from L. to R.: Mrs. L. E. Hilsden, Mrs. M. K. Abrahams, E. A. Godfrey, T. M. Scotney, F. W. Figg, C. F. Tebbutt, Lady D. Shepperson, M. J. Allen, C. G. Argles (Vice-Chairman), The Rt. Hon. The Earl of Sandwich, W. Brown (Chairman), J. B. Kelly (Clerk of the Council), The Rt. Hon. Lord De Ramsey, G. P. Radford, A. Crane, R. L. Farley, A. W. Blake, J. H. Moss, W. Ingram, Rev. M. H. Wells, N. F. Boyes.

58 The Huntingdonshire County Council photographed in 1952 in front of the 1899 Grammar School building. When the school moved to Brampton Road in 1939 the County Council occupied the premises. The building was demolished to make way for the headquarters of Anglian Water. The roundel visible beneath the central pinnacle has been preserved in the boundary wall of the Anglian headquarters.

59 Councillors and officers of the corporation photographed against the bow window of the library of Hinchingbrooke House between 1896-1898. The mayor, the 8th Earl of Sandwich, sits between the four aldermen and the sergeant at mace, Matthew Burton.

60 Men of the Huntingdon Fire Brigade in 1900. In the 18th century the town acquired two manual fire engines, one supplied by the Sun Fire Office and one by the Royal Exchange. The engine house stood in front of St Bennet's churchyard, but was demolished to open up the entrance to St Benedict's Court. Note the leather buckets once demanded of new burgesses.

61 The 1890 Fire Brigade is drawn up in front of the Town Hall. At this time the exterior of the hall was rendered to simulate Portland stone, and the ground floor colonnades on the Princes Street frontage were not enclosed. The ladder reaches to the window of the 1817 tea room extension to the 1745 assembly room.

62 A fire on the corner of St Clement's Passage or Mutton Lane. During the rebuilding a new shop was constructed for Danns and Chandler (see plate 98).

Churches and Schools

Before the Black Death, Huntingdon contained 16 parish churches, nine of which were owned by the Austin priory of St Mary. In addition to the priory the town possessed an Augustinian friary and the Hospital of St John. At Hinchingbrooke there was a Benedictine nunnery and at the Spittals the Hospital of St Margaret. Seventeen religious houses beyond the boundaries of Huntingdon, and in some cases beyond Huntingdonshire, also had property in town. At the Dissolution the religious houses and hospitals passed into secular hands. In the Civil War campaigns of 1645 two of the four remaining churches were damaged and were eventually demolished, leaving the two churches which exist today. The dissenting nonconformist tradition took strong roots in the town, George Fox 'was received very lovingly by the mayor' in 1656, and John Wesley preached in the town in 1780. Replacing inadequate buildings, large churches were erected for the Congregationalists/Baptists in 1867 and for the Methodists in 1878.

Oliver Cromwell and Samuel Pepys attended Huntingdon Grammar School which had emerged in the 16th century from the Hospital of St John. In the 17th century the rôles of the Master of the Hospital, of the mayor and burgesses and of the school master were specified but in 1836 and again in 1895 affairs were unsatisfactory and it was considered necessary to reform the organisation. The St John Hospital and Grammar School Foundation of 1895 absorbed the Charity School founded by Lionel Walden in 1736. It is interesting to note that money 'to clothe in green coats, braces and breeches, the boys attending Walden's school' was subsequently provided in 1760 by the charity established by Gabriel Newton. In 1625 Richard Fishborne of Huntingdon requested the Mercers' Company of London to use some of his funds for educational purposes in the town. In due course girls, also clothed in green, were supported and boys were apprenticed. Ultimately the money was used to support boys attending the Walden School and girls attending the National School. The grammar school moved from the town centre to Brampton Road and the pupils in their green uniforms are now at Hinchingbrooke, their third home. A British School was established in the old dissenting chapel, moving to Brookside in 1905 and eventually to St Peter's Road.

63 Huntingdon once possessed 16 churches owing allegiance to Rome. The present Church of St Michael the Archangel was built on the Hartford Road in 1901 and is now the only church in the town subscribing to 'the old faith'. This photograph was taken in 1901 presumably as a record of the previous structure that was about to be demolished.

64 This shows the Grammar School yard prior to 1868. When the Hospital of St John the Baptist was dissolved in 1547 it appears that the educational activity continued and in 1565 the Grammar School was officially established. The school master's house, to the right, dates from the 18th century.

65 The interior of the Grammar School after the 1878 reconstruction by Robert Hutchinson. The work was largely financed by Dion Boucicault in memory of his son who had been killed in the Abbots Ripton rail disaster of 1876. The result was the greater exposure of the original 12th-century structure erected by King David of Scotland.

66 Pupils and staff of the Grammar School photographed in 1911 with Mr. Howgate the headmaster. To the left can be seen the high wall which at that time still enclosed the yard. Three years later the Highland Mounted Brigade arrived with their horses to take temporary possession of the sports field.

67 This dissenting chapel constructed in 1826 was enlarged in the 1850s. From shortly after 1868, when the congregation moved to Trinity Church, through to 1905 the chapel became the British School. This photograph was taken in 1873. The County Record Office has been located here since 1974. The 1851 Sunday School building beyond is now Miguel's Café Bar.

68 A proposal to build 'The Cromwell Memorial Chapel' close to All Saints church was considered 'ostentatiously antagonistic'. The nonconformist church was therefore erected on the site of *The Dolphin* in the High Street. The first wedding in 'Trinity Church' took place in 1868 between Frederick Tarring, the son of the architect, and Eliza, daughter of Bateman Brown.

69 One hundred years after Thomas Coote placed the memorial stone in position in the High Street the congregation decided to sell the site of their 'nonconformist cathedral' to Tesco. The capital obtained was used to build New Trinity Church in Buttsgrove Way, better to serve the community as the town expanded beyond the old boundary.

70 On 22 May 1878 Bateman Brown, mayor of Huntingdon, and James Freshfield, mayor of Godmanchester, set in place the foundation stones of the Methodist Church designed by Mr. Hutchinson. To seat 600 persons the church replaced one erected 67 years earlier that in turn had replaced the 1779 chapel in which John Wesley had preached.

71 The Salvation Army was founded in 1865 by William Booth who 'saw no reason why the devil should have the best tunes'. This photograph shows the Godmanchester Army Band of 1892. The only person unable to remain stationary for the camera was the young boy!

72 Another group that presumably shared Booth's views was the choir of St Mary's Church, Huntingdon. The choir was photographed at the turn of the century, in front of the west door of the church, with the Reverend Henry Jackson.

73 Mrs. Emmelt and her girls photographed in the early 1880s. Mr. Whitney has written on one of the prints, 'Huntingdon teenagers, All Saints Church'.

74 St John the Evangelist was built on the site of the old theatre by Lady Olivia Bernard Sparrow in 1845. The church was not consecrated until 1866 because she insisted that the living should remain in her own hands. For a while communion was taken with the dissenters in the old chapel. The church was declared redundant in 1925.

Trade and Commerce

In his account of the Borough of Huntingdon, William Page in the *Victoria County History* noted that the Abbot of Ramsey's fair at St Ives had been pre-eminent until the mid-14th century and that Huntingdon was not the trading centre of the shire. However in the 10th century Huntingdon was already a market town and the home of a mint that functioned between the 10th and the 12th centuries. Merchants and traders supplied the needs of a sizeable population. The town held the public weights and measures, one of which was a measure of corn known as 'the common ring of Huntingdon'. The town possessed a water mill and there were four windmills. The coaching trade in the 18th century gave rise to the development of a number of inns to accommodate the growing volume of travellers.

During the period in which the majority of these photographs were taken, commercial river transport and milling finally declined and railway transport was rationalised. The town was engaged in metal working and in the construction of carriages, cars and aircraft. Gramophones and their records were produced. The brewery associated with the Cromwells amalgamated with the larger Huntingdon Brewery. The Huntingdon Brewery site has since been developed to provide shops and offices. The nursery and plant business of Wood and Ingram exported the Huntingdon elm and rose trees to Canada. The firm also supplied lime trees to stand alongside some of the thoroughfares in Huntingdon and trees for Grosvenor Square in London. Many of the shops along the High Street seemed to be owned by families who were members of Trinity church or who were associated with the church. However most of these small family businesses were unable to compete with the larger national chains and one by one they ceased to trade. These days the busy High Street contains the local branches of numerous national retailers. This trend was set as early as the 1890s by firms such as Freeman, Hardy and Willis, who are still trading, as 'Shoe Express', from a site acquired more than 100 years ago.

75 In 1893 Leonard Simpson acquired the navigation rights to the Great Ouse and established the Ouse Transport Company. Heavy goods were brought up river and agricultural produce sent down to King's Lynn. Beyond the lighters is the 15th-century chapel of St Ledger on the bridge at St Ives. The 18th-century upper floors were removed in 1930.

76 Huntingdon often complained that the watermills hindered the passage of vessels to the detriment of the Borough. One of the offenders was the mill of the Abbot of Ramsey at Houghton. In the 19th century three water-wheels were used to power 10 sets of stones. This mill is now in the care of the National Trust.

77 In 1499 John Stokes acquired the lease of the mill at Godmanchester with the provision that his wife should not visit the mill for the purpose of interfering with machinery! One pair of stones was set inside for the poor of the parish to use at no charge. The mill was demolished in 1927.

78 The Corporation Mill at Huntingdon was on a tributary of the Ouse. The inhabitants were compelled to make use of the mill and the income was used to pay the king's annual fee farm rent. In the middle distance can be seen the race-course grandstand, last used in 1896. These buildings no longer exist.

79 This photograph of the 1906 regatta is included to show the mills across the river in Godmanchester. Beyond the 1332 stone bridge is the Veasey Mill, constructed in the 1850s to produce oil and cattle cake. The building has been converted for residential use. Further round is the Brown and Goodman steam mill of 1861, now demolished.

80 Workmen at the Brown and Goodman mill, pictured in 1899. When the owners built the mill they acquired the latest machinery from France to construct an automatic mill. Ultimately this inland business could not compete with the flour mills established at the ports where the bulk grain ships were unloaded.

81 Originally the mills processed home-grown wheat. This 1938 photograph shows one of the early combine harvesters in the county. Drawn by an International 10/20 tractor the combine had a 12-foot cut. Mr. Leslie Seaton of Great Raveley drives, assisted by Mr. Harden of St Ives and Mr. Bosworth of Wood Walton. Mr. Bolton of International is on the left.

HUNTINGDON'S
LAST BIG FREEZE

PORTHOLME

82 *(above)* The railways linked the producers with the consumers; shown above is the twin track of the Joint Great Northern and Great Eastern railway crossing the river Ouse on the wooden trestle bridge constructed in the 1880s. Trapped in the ice beyond are the holiday house-boats. The high level A14 now crosses the river at this point.

83 *(above right)* Number 2750, The Flying Scotsman, speeds northwards. The first train on the Great Northern line passed through Huntingdon in 1850. Had plans to built the railway workshops in Huntingdon been successful, the town might have replaced Peterborough as the industrial centre of the region.

84 *(right)* The potential for industrial development existed in Huntingdon at the end of the last century. This photograph taken near the old Police Headquarters shows a works outing from the Iron Foundry.

85 This part of the town housed another industrial enterprise which might have grown to greater things, namely that of the Portholme Aerodrome Limited founded in 1911. This 1916 photograph shows a Wight seaplane type 840 under construction. The company also built Sopwith Snipes and Camels and its successor was eventually bought out by Handley Page Limited.

86 In 1911 James Radley, one of the Portholme Aerodrome partners, designed this gull-winged monoplane with its covered streamline body in marked contrast to the more open construction generally prevailing. He was the first person to fly a machine in the locality, becoming airborne over Portholme in 1910. He held the Royal Aero Club Certificate No. 12.

87 Radley's partner Will Moorhouse, holder of the Royal Aero Club Certificate No. 147, flew from Portholme. Will is shown in 1912 at the wheel of the car transporting his Bleriot. Marshall Brothers have obviously seen the advertising potential. Will was mortally wounded on a bombing mission in 1915 and became the first airman to be awarded the Victoria Cross.

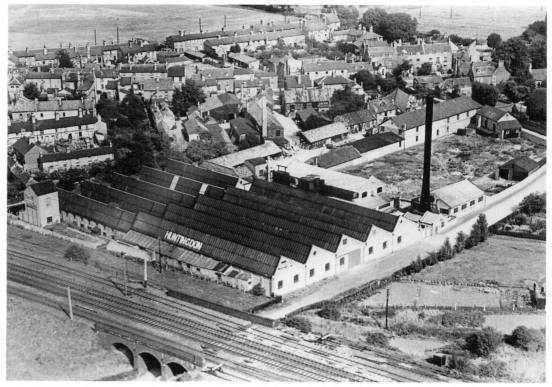

88 This locality off Handcroft Lane is one of the early industrial areas of Huntingdon. Here or close by were the premises of the foundry, of Portholme Limited and of Eddison Bell, manufacturers of gramophones and gramophone records between 1923 and 1930. The present occupier of this site, Standard Products Limited, makes rubber mouldings for the motor car industry.

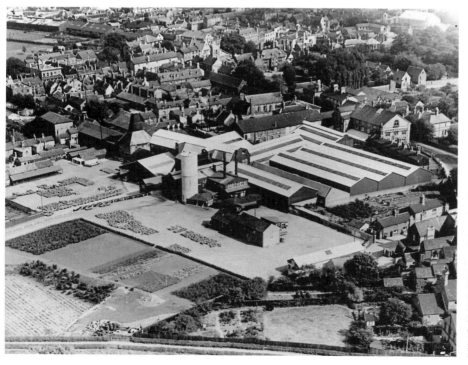

89 Between George Street and St John's Street was another industrial area. From 1860 until 1924 the carriage works of Charles Sandford Windover were here. From 1930 there was the vegetable processing works of Chivers and Sons Limited, which was acquired by Batchelors Foods in 1959. The site has been redeveloped and is now occupied by the George Street Industrial Estate and Godwin House.

90 Windovers produced carriages for royalty at home and overseas. This carriage with its folding hood was photographed in 1912, when the market for horse-drawn carriages was in decline. The skills of the coach builders, however, had already been redirected to the automobile.

91 Photographed by the young Mr. Whitney in 1907 outside The Cottage, the 8th Earl sits in his Daimler landaulet car with Mr. Woodbine his driver and Mr. Abbot his valet. The car is believed to be carrying the Huntingdonshire number plate EW1. The Cottage is now the headquarters of the Cambridgeshire Fire and Rescue Service.

92 Murkett Brothers' St Mary's cycle and motor works of 22, High Street photographed in the late 1890s. One of their products was the Hunting Don cycle. Now with facilities on Brookside and Stukeley Road, the firm previously operated from other premises in the High Street including *The Fountain*. Early hangers from Wyton were re-erected on the Brookside site. Photograph courtesy of Mr. D. Murkett.

93 At the funeral of George Maddox in 1921 all but one of the cars in the procession were Maddox vehicles lent by their owners for the occasion. The works, which were destroyed by fire three years later, are visible on the right.

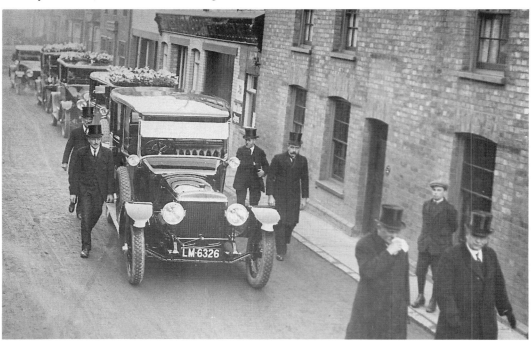

94 & 95 These pictures printed from lantern slides show the harvesting of potatoes produced by Charles Papworth of Hartford. In 1905 he grew 200 different types produced by cross fertilisation. Some plants were five feet from root to tip and one seed produced 11 pounds of tubers. He harvested four tons of strawberries in 1905, perhaps including these which are being gathered in the Mill Road area of Hartford.

96 This photograph of 1894 records the building of the short-lived west wing to Hinchingbrooke House. The wing was destroyed in 1974. The men are shown with the tools of their craft: the bricklayers display their trowels, the carpenters their saws.

HANDS OF
THE POTTER

FEN POTTERIES
HUNTINGDON

97 When the Ermine Street studio ceased to serve the photographic business it was used by the Fen Potteries. Amongst the rubble and broken glass in the cellar there were several intact beakers very similar to the one being thrown on the wheel.

98 Photographed in 1907 after the fire. What became of Mazawattee cocoa? Fins Aquatic Centre currently occupies these premises.

99 Before the supermarkets arrived. This may be the interior of the Danns and Chandler shops prior to the fire. Even if this identification is incorrect, the photograph warrants close examination just to discover familiar brand names. Who remembers bargain broken biscuits sold from the tins?

100 Candles to methylated spirits, lamps, mats, baskets and distemper were all available at Pirkis's Store, photographed in 1911—even dog food! 122 High Street is now the home of W.H. Smith and Argos.

101 This is identified in the index of the collection as Coxon's the haberdashery and was photographed in 1925. It would therefore now be incorporated into Burton's shop.

102 Edward Henry Fisher, born in St Ives, spent some years overseas before returning to Huntingdon in 1898. His shop, photographed in 1904, stood at the corner of the High Street and Grammar School Walk. For many years the site of Boots the Chemist, it is now the offices of the Leeds Permanent Building Society.

103 Fisher's modified the premises once used by R.W. Woolley to create these island display windows and other windows alongside the entrance to The Hippodrome cinema. These buildings were demolished in the 1970s and in their place are now Boots the Chemist and the Wimpy restaurant.

104 Photographed in 1892, this shows Freeman Hardy and Willis Limited relocated from north of *The George Hotel*. This site was the former premises of the Pasheller's bank that had failed in 1827.

105 From 1899, when for most people 'horsepower' would have meant precisely that, H. Peacock, Saddler & Harness Maker, occupied 103 High Street, now the premises of Black Horse Agencies, January's the estate agents.

106 By now horsepower was beginning to mean something else, and here we have G. Miller in his Daimler. The photograph was taken in 1911 in the yard of *The George Hotel* with Mary Jane Fisher, the proprietor. She subsequently purchased the hotel from the Duke of Manchester.

107 The providers of financial advice, life assurance and insurance against loss would have found many clients in the county town. Huntingdon, with its Corn Exchange and many banks, was a financial centre. These Prudential agents were photographed in 1894.

108 Mr. and Mrs. Binge with their shell-fish barrow in Ferrars Road in 1909. I understand that Mr. Binge was the last town crier of Huntingdon. This photograph has been used in a booklet written to introduce schoolchildren to life at the beginning of this century. The inner ring road now cuts across the middle ground.

Personalities

In the early days of portrait photography the sitter was required to maintain a pose for a long time and this was made possible by the use of a clamp to hold the head stationary; Mrs. Parsons faced the camera for three minutes! Later, as photographic technology improved, it became possible to produce 'snap shot' portraits such as the one of the boatman dealing with his customers by the bridge. The superb quality of many of these early negatives enables us to produce excellent high definition prints more than 125 years after the photographs were taken. Wedding days have always been occasions for families to gather together and photographs taken on the day have made it possible for us many years later to observe the fashions worn by the bride and groom and their guests. We can eavesdrop on such scenes as the 1870s' wedding breakfast laid out beneath the banners proclaiming 'English Maidens Pure and Lovely'. As with the individual portrait, the family portrait could be formal or captured by snap shot. In the latter category is the photograph of a family of travellers taken by Ernest Whitney alongside the road between Thrapston and Huntingdon. In Victorian and Edwardian times it seems that the servants of affluent families were often photographed as groups. Occasionally, an individual servant was recorded carrying out his or her function; for example, the groom with the horse at Hartford or the chauffeur with the new-fangled automobile in Huntingdon.

109 Edward George Henry, 8th Earl of Sandwich, 1839-1916 photographed in 1890. The Earl was the first chairman of the Huntingdonshire County Council in 1888. Between 1858 and 1875 he undertook various diplomatic missions and entertained Edward VII at Hinchingbrooke in 1906. The Earl did not marry and was succeeded by his nephew.

110 Doctor J.T. Baumgartner was the Hon. Physician of the Dispensary and Infirmary that had been established on the Walks in 1789 and 1831 respectively. Although he had moved to Milton near Cambridge, he continued in office when the new Infirmary was constructed and equipped for just under £8,000 in 1854. The photograph predates 1867.

111 The Reverend James Henry Millard, 1819-83, succeeded his father-in-law The Reverend William Wright as pastor of the old chapel from 1846 until 1858, and then became minister of New Trinity until 1877. A man full of nonconformist zeal, his influence was strongly felt in Huntingdon. At one time he was the curator of the museum in the Literary and Scientific Institution. He was the secretary of the Baptist Union, 1863-77. Photographed c.1878.

112 The nonchalant onlooker in his blazer adds to the atmosphere of this river scene. The figure of the boatman with his pole makes a fine subject for this lantern slide; he is believed to be Mr. Bitten of Adelaide Terrace, Godmanchester.

113 *(top left)* This portrait of a Victorian lady was taken in the 1870s. The subject resting upon the back of the chair is Mrs. R. Ashton who lived at 1 Walks North, Huntingdon.

114 *(above)* This wet plate negative was formed on a sheet of glass 12 inches by 9¼ inches. It is inscribed 'Mrs Parsons of Elsworth, exposed 3 minutes, bright day, triplex lens'. Photographed before 1867; although Mrs. Parsons was probably supported by a neck clamp, she was unable to prevent the movement of the book held in her right hand.

115 *(left)* This splendid portrait taken in the Bedford studio before 1867 is that of Mary 'The Flying Duchess', the wife of the 11th Duke of Bedford. She made record-breaking flights to India and to South Africa in 1929 and 1930. The Duchess was a keen photographer. She died in 1937 when her aircraft crashed into the sea near Yarmouth; her body was not recovered.

116 Mr. and Mrs. Bateman Brown on their golden wedding anniversary in 1898. Bateman, born in Houghton in 1823, moved into Huntingdon in 1863. A partner in the Brown and Goodman mill, he was a staunch nonconformist and helped to finance the local dissenting cause. He became mayor of Huntingdon and a Justice of the Peace.

117 Photographed in the 1870s, this picture is listed as the Davies' wedding breakfast. The banners arching between the vines in the conservatory read 'English Maidens pure and lovely' and 'God Bless the Union'.

118   In the late 1870s Philip Tillard, the eldest son of Philip Tillard of Stukeley Hall, married Iona Bonham Carter. Philip became a barrister and a Justice of the Peace. He was a senior partner in the Huntingdon Bank of Veasey and Desborough and Co., which eventually merged into Barclays Bank.

119   Guests at the wedding included the Duke and Duchess of Manchester, General and Mrs. Baumgartner, Mr. and Mrs. Philip Tillard Snr. and the Reverends Woodruff and Rooper.

120 This photograph was taken in 1879-80 and is identified as 'Mr and Mrs Burnaby wedding group'. The Burnabys resided at The Manor House in Brampton, a building later used by the police and now part of the Cheshire Foundation.

121 A more modest wedding group, 'The Livetts', was photographed in the 1880s in front of what is now 24 Main Street, Hartford.

122 *(top left)* Included for its intrinsic appeal, Mrs. Woodford and her grandchildren were photographed in 1891. I believe that the Woodfords once lived in Hartford Road.

123 *(above)* Another family believed once to have lived in Hartford Road were the Tysoes. This photograph taken in 1900 is identified as 'Tysoes—four generation group'.

124 *(left)* The Montagu family at Hinchingbrooke in the 1930s. The 9th Earl holds the dog, Gillie, behind him is Lady Olga Montagu, and to her left the Hon. Drogo Montagu and Lord Hinchingbrooke. The young girl is Lady Elizabeth and looking from the window is the Countess of Sandwich.

125 Mr. Whitney was returning to Huntingdon from Thrapston and saw this family alongside the road. He was entitled to be pleased with the resultant photograph. A scene not likely to be reproduced now that the road has been upgraded as the A14, A1-M1 link road!

126 No doubt these members of the domestic staff at Hinchingbrooke in 1906 considered that they were occupying prestigious positions in the big house of the county town. In a similar group taken in 1909, the staff had increased to 35 in number.

127 At Stukeley Hall in the 1870s the Tillards gave employment to these 18 people photographed outside the coach house. The coach house has been given a new lease of life as a private residence.

128 Great Stukeley Park was created by the Torkington family at the time of the parliamentary enclosure in 1816, taking in part of Moorfield and parcels of land possessed by St John's and Trinity Colleges in Cambridge. The Torkingtons also closed the way between Owls End and Green End. These flower beds in the lawn were photographed in the late 1870s.

129 A more modest domestic group in the service of the Reverend Frederick Ripley of Hartford. They were photographed in June 1880; the groom stands behind the model horse on the table. At this time the Reverend Ripley looked after about 440 parishioners.

130 The groom in livery steadies the Reverend Ripley's horse with Master Ripley aboard, photographed in 1880.

131 A change in uniform. Here we have Mr. Woods of Temple Close, Orchard Lane, the chauffeur in charge of Bateman Brown's Marot-Gardon powered by a 2½-horse power De Dion engine. Originally constructed in France as a four-wheeled vehicle, it has been converted into a tricycle, photographed in 1902.

Recreation

It is not surprising to find that the Whitney collection contains photographs of townsfolk enjoying themselves on the river. There are many images of people just messing about on the water, but in contrast there are also photographs of serious sportsmen such as the four oarsmen with their cox recorded in 1901. Similarly, in the shire town of a largely agricultural community it is not surprising to discover photographs of people shooting, hunting or fishing. Sports teams were frequent subjects and reproduced in this section are cricket and football teams from 1893 and members of a tennis club, *c.*1905. Leisure time provided an opportunity for continued education beyond normal schooling, a process greatly encouraged by the schools and by the churches through their various clubs and societies. Photographs of uniformed organisations include those showing Scouts and Guides and The Church Lads Brigade. Some of the early photographs show the boys being drilled in a military fashion that would probably be unacceptable these days. More unusual leisure time pursuits are shown such as a man racing against a donkey cart and 'the finish of a marathon race' from Ramsey to Huntingdon in aid of the county hospital funds. Also chosen for this section are photographs of a fun fair from the turn of the century and of a 1930s' town carnival.

132 A tranquil river scene looking upstream from the meadows alongside Newtown. At this time many properties in Temple Close and Orchard Lane extended down to the river bank. Following the construction of the Ring Road, it is now possible to walk from the bridge through the riverside park and the meadows to Hartford church.

133 A coxed four, photographed in 1901. The Huntingdon Boat Club premises lay across the river from the castle but today are to be found on the other side of the river near the car park servicing the riverside park.

134 Great excitement: a large fish believed to be a sturgeon has been sighted! This photograph shows attempts being made to capture the fish at Hemingford. I understand that on this occasion the large public gathering was disappointed and the fish escaped!

135 However, as is evident from this lantern slide, a sturgeon was landed from the Great Ouse. I understand that the man with both hands on the fish was Mr. Bryant.

136 Also reproduced from a lantern slide, this photograph taken by Mr. Whitney pleased him for the sharpness of the image of the diver in flight. Was this a supervised swim or just boys having fun?

137 A picnic group on the meadows. Frederick Hinde and his mother, Mrs. Maddison, with friends from Trinity Church enjoy the outdoor life together.

138 James Smart of Welney and Hendrick Lindahl of Redditch, photographed in 1894. The deliberate flooding of the meadows alongside the river gave rise to an ideal skating venue in the winter. James Smart was the European champion speed skater 1890-1—for 'European' read 'English and Dutch'!

139 There are few natural inclines in Huntingdon suitable for tobogganing. This man-made slope was created when the castle was constructed in 1068. The folk enjoying the snow were photographed in 1878. A windmill previously occupied the summit of the motte.

140 Leisure activity in a different league, with the Prince of Wales and party gathered at Kimbolton Castle for a Hunt meeting. The group was photographed outside the salon in the 1860s.

141 Photographed in 1893, this shows another traditional countryside pursuit. Mr. Hodgson and his shooting party are shown equipped with their double-barrelled sporting guns.

142 'Before the darts came', patrons of pubs used to enjoy themselves playing quoits. This photograph was taken in 1898 at *The Barley Mow* in Hartford. The player is believed to be Mr. Childs.

143 Members of the Hartford debating class of 1910-11 are gathered in the old school, presumably developing the arts of logical argument and of public speaking.

144 Acting for the Earl of Sandwich, Robert Hutchinson designed Newtown and 82 plots of land for residential development were auctioned by G.M. Fox at *The George Hotel* on 27 April 1860. In due course the Newtown Albion Football Club arrived on the scene and here is the team photographed in 1893.

145 The 2nd eleven of Huntingdon Cricket Club in 1893. Frederick Hinde in his blazer stands between the two umpires, the one on his right is Morton Lewin, surveyor of the highways to the rural district council. Seated between them is Mr. W.H. Ellwood, the captain.

146 The Trinity Church tennis club of c.1905. Mr. Whitney has identified members of the group and it is noticeable that many would seem to be, or were related to, owners of the retail businesses in Huntingdon.

147 Competitors ran 18 miles from Ramsey church via St Ives to Hinchingbrooke Park. The winner, 28-year-old William Lawrence of Stilton, completed the race in just under two hours. The Earl of Sandwich presents the silver trophy donated by Oliver Locker Lampson, the prospective unionist candidate. The event was organised to raise funds for the county hospital in 1909.

148 It seems that a race, starting at *The King of the Belgians* in Hartford, was organised between a donkey and cart and the gentleman wearing the 'V' emblazoned shirt.

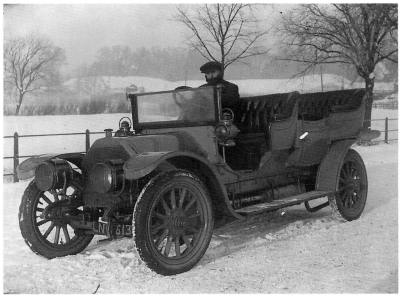

149 Open-air motoring with a vengeance. Mr. Eyre in his Weigel, photographed in 1908; the coach-building tradition is still evident in the design of the body. In the distance can be seen the earthworks of Huntingdon Castle.

150 Many young people in Huntingdon were inspired by Lieutenant General Robert Baden-Powell and Olave, his wife, to spend their leisure time as scouts and guides. The movements encourage the development of the physical and spiritual well-being of their members and foster international understanding. The founders are shown at Hinchingbrooke House.

151 Barker and Thurston have arrived on Mill Common with the carousel, swing boats and coconut shies. Trinity spire rises above the trees. It is possible that some of the younger boys came from Edward House, which had been established by the Earl of Sandwich on the far side of the common.

152 A country cottage followed by a fire engine approaches the Hartford Road between *The Three Tuns* and St Mary's vicarage. Other vehicles in the carnival procession line the High Street. The AA signs on the wall of *The Three Tuns* point to St Ives, to Ely, to Ramsey and Chatteris.

Events and National Politics

The impact of national politics and of national events upon the life of the town has been referred to on many of the preceding ages. The town of Huntingdon returned two Members of Parliament until 1868 when the representation was reduced to one. The burgesses of Huntingdon at first maintained the right to nominate and choose two from their corporate body. Robert Cromwell and his son Oliver were both returned for the borough in the 16th century. Oliver was 29 years of age when elected and three years later he moved away from the town. He held supreme political office on the national scene as 'The Lord Protector' from the age of 54 until his death five years later. In time it became usual for the Lord Lieutenant to nominate potential candidates with the burgesses choosing the members. This eventually evolved to a situation whereby the Sandwich family controlled the nomination of candidates, sometimes advancing non-burgesses and sometimes acting in consideration for payment. Between 1660 and 1882 there were 50 'elections' and of these 40 were not contested. Those in opposition were unable to mount a campaign that stood a realistic chance of defeating the Sandwich interest. Sandwich protégés included Lancelot Brown, the son of Capability Brown, and William Fellowes from Ramsey.

Affairs were more complicated at the county level, which also returned two Members. Here there were often contests between the 'Tory' Sandwich faction and the 'Whig' Manchesters. For a brief period in the 1820s Lord John Russell was one of the Huntingdonshire Members of Parliament. More recent times have seen David Renton, now the Lord Renton, representing the interests of Huntingdonshire in the Lower House for 34 years, with another 16 years' service in the Upper Chamber. The Member of Parliament for Huntingdonshire elected in 1979 became the British Prime Minister in 1990. John Major has joined his predecessor Oliver Cromwell in shouldering the responsibility for the management of the nations' political affairs; albeit in a greatly changed state.

Photographs in this section relate to events or scenes in Huntingdon that perhaps more directly reflect national events. There are photographs showing local celebrations at Queen Victoria's Golden and Diamond Jubilees and at the Silver Jubilee of George V. The local proclamations of George VI and of Queen Elizabeth II are captured. Huntingdon's involvement with the Crimean War, the Boer War and the First and Second World Wars are the subjects of other pictures. Photographs of a political interest include those of Stanley Baldwin, of George Lansbury and of Sir David Renton.

153 This trophy was taken during the Crimean War. The original cannon was removed in the Second World War for recycling. During the Gulf War John Major unveiled the replica which now stands on the stone-plinth. Beyond can be seen the Chivers factory and, alongside, some of the eight almshouses erected *c*.1852 as part of the St John's Hospital Charity.

154 The Hunts Militia photographed in May 1872 in their rifle green uniforms, 'the colour of the county', according to Mr. Bird in his 1911 reminiscences. At first the headquarters and stores were in *The Falcon Inn* but in the 1850s these barracks at Brookside were constructed. In 1854 the complement was over 400 officers and men. The barracks are now the Cromwell Square residences.

155 Queen Victoria's Golden Jubilee in 1887. To the right can be seen *The Fountain Hotel*; the archway led into the courtyard and to the Corn Exchange, later the Grand Cinema. Alongside is Pashellar's, now Shoe Express. The sign to the left of the union flag reads, 'Visit Hendry's Art Studio'. This photograph, much enlarged, is displayed in the Tesco Supermarket alongside the northern bypass.

156 Queen Victoria' Diamond Jubilee in 1897 was celebrated throughout the county. Here in Hemingford Grey we have an alfresco meal. At the top table facing the camera are Mrs. Herbert and the Reverend Henry Herbert, the great-grandparents of the present Lord Hemingford. To Mrs. Herbert's left is Colonel Sholto Douglas, the lord of the manor.

157 This 1889 photograph shows the unveiling of the drinking water fountain erected in the memory of the 7th Earl of Sandwich. The 7th Earl commissioned Blore to rebuild the north-east corner of Hinchingbrooke House following the 1830 fire. The terracotta fountain by Eddis no longer exists.

158 In 1899 the town commemorated the birth of its most remarkable son. Oliver Cromwell was baptised in St John's Church and attended the Grammar School. A Member of Parliament for Huntingdon in 1628-29, he moved away in 1630. Following the conflicts of the civil war he became Lord Protector of the Commonwealth of England, Scotland and Ireland from 1653 until his death in 1658.

159 Photographed in 1901, these are men of the Hunts Volunteer Battalion. In 1908 the Huntingdonshire battalion was disbanded and men joined the 5th Battalion of the Bedfordshire Regiment. The Huntingdonshire Territorial Cyclist Battalion was established in 1914.

160 At a time when the bicycle had given many people independent mobility it is not surprising to find that the celebration to mark the end of the Boer War in 1902 takes the form of a fancy dress cycle parade with both riders and vehicles suitably decorated.

161 Miss Montagu re-enacts Queen Elizabeth visiting Hinchingbrooke House in 1564. The 9th Earl, introducing this 1912 pageant, said: '... lend your swift imagination and we will make jump to your eye the ghosts of other days, Kings, Queens, Knights, courtiers and simples who have trod, as we tread now, this plot of ground'.

162 Past events were recalled in another way by these Hartford youngsters recreating the ancient Plough Witching Ceremony. On the second Monday of January the plough boys used to blacken their faces, wear their coats inside out or dress up as women. Drawing their plough and singing customary songs they would then visit households expecting to be given money.

163 This incredible document was presented in the field in May 1916 to Captain Roxby of the No. 10 Kite Balloon section of the Royal Flying Corp on the occasion of his birthday. The illuminated address prepared by S. Sweeting bears the signatures of 97 of his fellow officers and men.

164 Members of 42 Squadron pose alongside their open cockpit De Havilland DH9 aircraft; their uniform is clearly still evolving. Wyton, first opened in 1916, has seen many changes. Continuing the long-standing local connection with aviation, Wyton now houses the logistics headquarters of the Royal Air Force.

MRS PROBY LORD SANDWICH STANLEY BALDWIN PRIME MINISTER MRS BALDWIN HINCH. LADY MONTAGUE MAJOR PROBY AT HINCHINGBROOK ABOUT 1926

165 Victor Montagu, the 9th Earl's son, succeeded to the title in 1962 and had to relinquish his seat in the House of Commons. In 1964 he gave up the title but failed to be re-elected. He had been Assistant Private Secretary to Stanley Baldwin, photographed here at Hinchingbrooke House in 1926. Baldwin was the British Prime Minister on three occasions. Victor sold Hinchingbrooke to the County Council in 1962.

166 George Lansbury addresses a gathering at Alconbury. As First Commissioner of Public Works, he was a cabinet minister and later the leader of the socialist party in opposition. He was an ardent pacifist who lived to see the outbreak of the Second World War. He died in 1940 at the age of 81 years.

167 Assembled for the Silver Jubilee of King George V on 6 May 1935 are voluntary organisations, including the guides with Miss P. Goodliff as one of the leaders. On the platform dignitaries include the Earl of Sandwich and Mayor E.A. Fisher. Free entertainment was provided in the Grand, also in The Hippodrome, and 800 children enjoyed a celebration tea.

168 This photograph is included to recall the privilege accorded to the Mayor of Godmanchester who announced the new Sovereign from horseback. Here in 1936 Alderman James proclaims George VI on the school hill. He also repeated the proclamation at the boundary on the centre of the bridge. The High Sheriff would normally be expected to make the announcement.

169 There was great fear, following the events in the First World War, that toxic gas would be used against the population in the Second World War. Hence a demonstration of the use of respirators or gas masks.

170 During the Second World War the Church of St John the Evangelist became a first-aid post, the entrance being protected against bomb blast by a wall of sand bags. Over 1,000 incendiary bombs were dropped on Huntingdon but the number of fatalities in the town was thankfully low. There were, of course, tragic losses of ground- and air-crew from the local airfields.

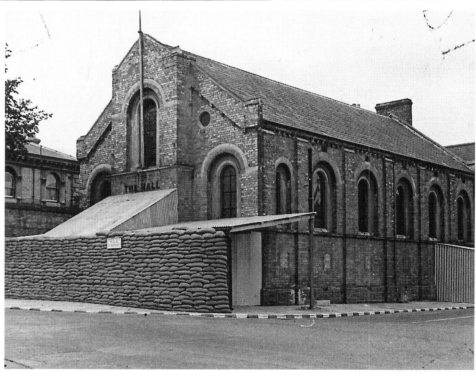

171 At the beginning of the Second World War RAF Alconbury was a satellite of RAF Wyton, housing Blenheim and Wellington bombers. Between 1942 and 1945 the USAAF flew Liberators and Flying Fortresses from the base. The USAF returned in 1951, and the runway was operational until March 1995. The photograph shows the construction of staff accommodation in the 1950s.

172 Mr. Whitney on the extreme left listens to the proclamation of Elizabeth II made by the Sheriff on the balcony of the Town Hall in 1952.

173 David Renton was a pupil as Oundle School, as was Ailwyn de Ramsey. During the Second World War Lord de Ramsey served in the Far East and Lord Renton served in Libya. Shown in this photograph, taken by the Huntingdon photographer Ron Bailey in the late 1970s, are the Reverend Arthur Brown, the Lord Lieutenant Lord de Ramsey, Lord Renton and Mr. Harry Raby, standing on a saluting platform in Walden Road.

174 Photographed during the 1974 election in Huntingdon are Sir David, now Lord, Renton, with his wife Paddy and Claire and Caroline, two of his daughters. Caroline holds the hand of her son David Dodds-Parker, the eldest grandchild. Lord Renton has served at Westminster for 50 years.